# THE GIRL WHO LOVED WORDS

This book belongs to

**Read more in the Dreamers series by Lavanya Karthik**

*The Girl Who Loved to Sing: Teejan Bai*

*The Boy Who Played with Light: Satyajit Ray*

*The Girl Who Was a Forest: Janaki Ammal*

*The Boys Who Created Malgudi: R.K. Narayan and R.K. Laxman*

*The Girl Who Climbed Mountains: Bachendri Pal*

*The Boy Who Loved Birds: Salim Ali*

*The Boy Who Made Magic: P.C. Sorcar*

# THE GIRL WHO LOVED WORDS

## MAHASWETA DEVI

Written and illustrated by

### LAVANYA KARTHIK

An imprint of Penguin Random House

For you and the words you cherish

DUCKBILL BOOKS

USA | Canada | UK | Ireland | Australia
New Zealand | India | South Africa | China | Singapore

Duckbill Books is part of the Penguin Random House group of companies
whose addresses can be found at global.penguinrandomhouse.com

Published by Penguin Random House India Pvt. Ltd
4th Floor, Capital Tower 1, MG Road,
Gurugram 122 002, Haryana, India

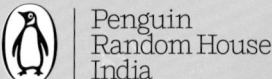

Penguin
Random House
India

First published in Duckbill Books by
Penguin Random House India 2022

Text and illustrations copyright © Lavanya Karthik 2022

ISBN 9780143458418

Typeset in Georgia by DiTech Publishing Services Pvt. Ltd
Printed at Paras Offset Pvt. Ltd., Kundli (Haryana)

www.penguin.co.in

Mahasweta Devi was a writer and activist who used her writing to fight injustice. Her novels and short stories describe the lives and struggles of India's tribal communities. But before she became a renowned Bangla writer, she was a little girl called Khuku who loved words.

This is her story.

'Tell us a story!' the children say.
'We can't sleep!'

'Hmmm,' says their older sister.
'Have you heard about Nyadosh,
Ma's meat-eating cow?'

'Yes, we have!'

'Should I tell you about your
brother Phalgu and the cheetah man?'

'We know that one too!'

'Well then, it is time I told you
about Khuku.'

Words were Khuku's first friends.

They called out to her from the
bookshelves of Ma and Baba's house.

They *danced* across the pages of the newspaper.

They *led* the way. Khuku followed.

'Still so tiny and she's learnt to read!' Baba was amazed.

'That's all she does!' Ma smiled. 'It's like she cannot stop.'

Words were windows, showing Khuku the world outside her home in Dhaka.

Words were colours, lighting up her dreams.

Words were friends . . .

Until they became knives.

'She's only ten!' Baba said. 'Why must we send her so far away to study?'

'She's a big girl!' said Ma. 'She needs a proper education.'

The words cut deep.

Khuku wept.

Khuku raged.

Yet, what could she do but obey?

On a cold day in December, Khuku began the long journey from Dhaka to a school called Santiniketan, near Calcutta.

Far from home, far from everyone
she knew, Khuku felt lost and alone.

Until new friends took her by the hand . . .

and old friends called to her again.

Three years flowed by, like the waters of the murmuring Kopai.

Years of happiness, at the school Khuku now called home.

Until words hurt her again.

'Come home for the holidays,' her aunt said. 'Meet your little brothers and sisters.'

Khuku travelled to Calcutta, where her family now lived.

'Your mother is ill,' said Baba. 'You must care for your siblings now. You will not be going back to Shantiniketan.'

Khuku raged.

Khuku wept.

Yet, what could she do but obey?

How would she care for her
brothers and sisters?

Once more, her old friends reached out.

'Would you like me to tell you a story?' Khuku asked.

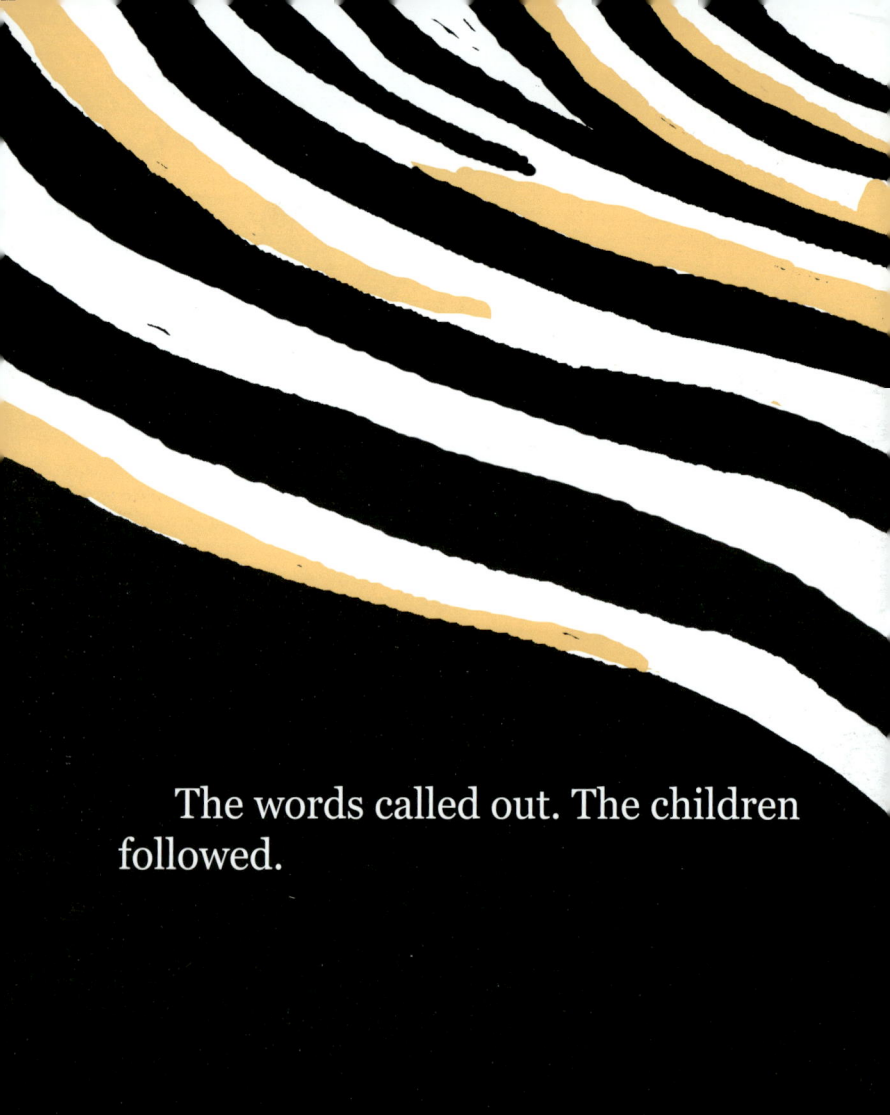

The words called out. The children followed.

Four years rushed by, like the waters of the mighty Hooghly

The year Khuku turned seventeen, famine raged across her world.

Crops were snatched away to feed British troops fighting in World War II. The streets of Calcutta were filled with the starving poor.

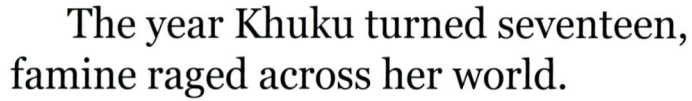

Khuku could not stand by. She went out each day, handing out food and water. Day after day, she returned, her head filled with images of the sick and dying, and the sounds of their cries for help.

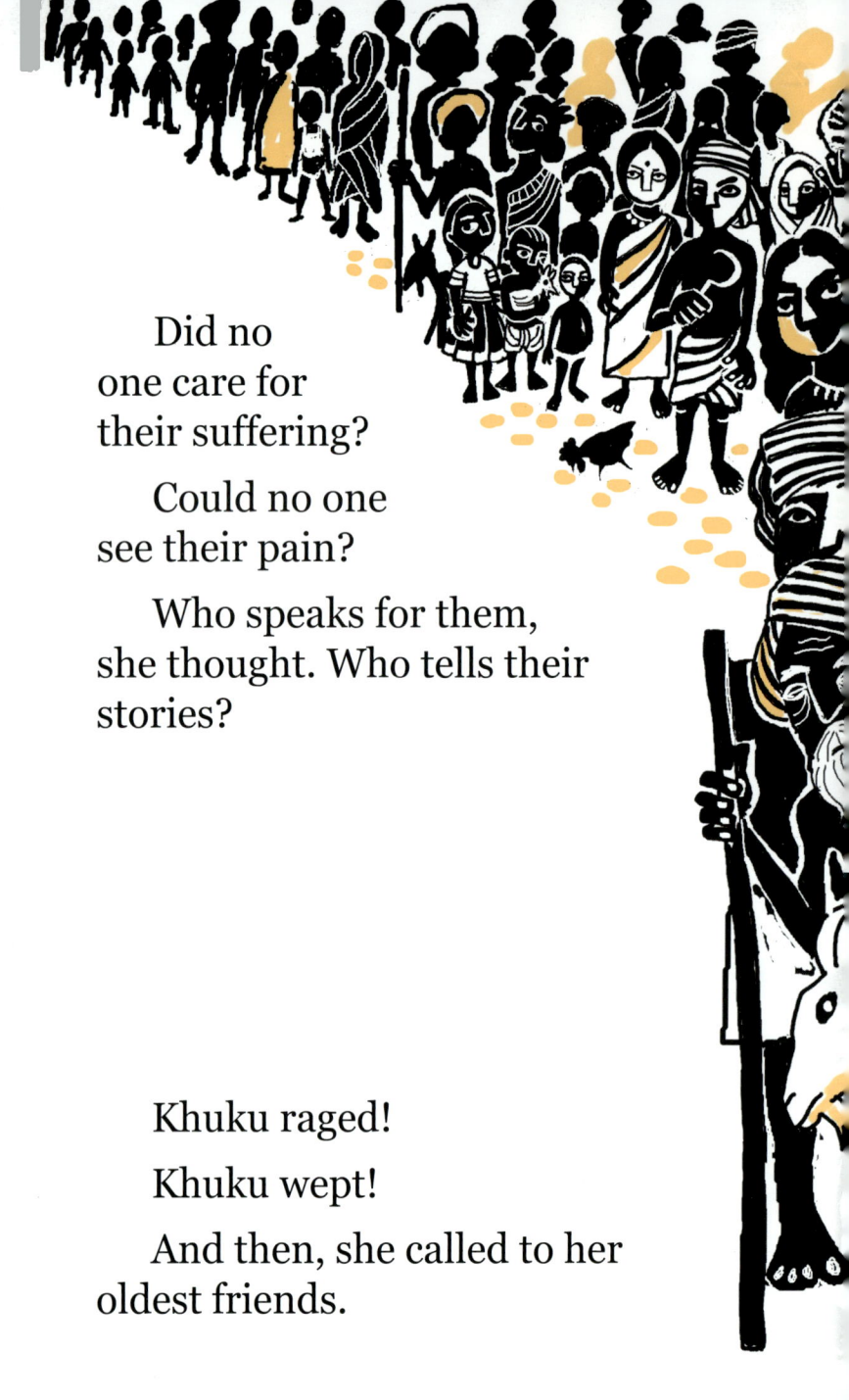

Did no
one care for
their suffering?

Could no one
see their pain?

Who speaks for them,
she thought. Who tells their
stories?

Khuku raged!

Khuku wept!

And then, she called to her
oldest friends.

Her words would tell their stories.
They would be—

  eyes that did not look away,

  voices that told of their
     suffering,

  fists raised in fury,
   hands claiming their
     share.

She picked up her pen.
The words followed.

The children are quiet.

'What happened next?' they ask.

'She began to write,' their sister says.

'And?'

*'I never stopped.'*

Mahasweta Devi (1926-2016) wrote over a hundred novels and many short stories, all of them focused on people Indian society mostly ignored.

She wrote about Adivasis and Dalits, and the suffering they faced at the hands of Indian and colonial rulers. She travelled to remote villages to live with the people there, understand their lives and tell their stories.

She was a journalist and an activist for human rights and devoted her life to improving conditions for the Indian poor and marginalised.

She was awarded a Padma Shri, a Padma Vibhushan, the Jnanpith and the Ramon Magsaysay Award.

*Artist Chittaprosad Bhattacharya (1915-1978) used his sketches and prints to voice the suffering of the millions affected by the Bengal Famine of 1943. The illustrations in this book are inspired by his work.*

The author wishes to thank
Ina Puri for her invaluable help
in the making of this book.

Lavanya Karthik is an author
and illustrator by day, a cookie
monster by teatime, and fast
asleep by nine at night. She
lives in Mumbai where she eats
a lot of chocolate and takes a lot
of naps.